Study Guide

Student Workbook for

The Spiderwick Chronicles

The Field Guide

By: Rowan Black

The <u>Black Student Workbooks</u> are designed to get students thinking critically about the text they read and provide a guided study format to facilitate in improved learning and retention. Teachers and Homeschool Instructors may use the activities included to improve student learning and organization.

Students will construct and identify the following areas of knowledge.

Character Identification

Events

Location

Vocabulary

Main Idea

Conflict

And more as appropriate to the text.

How to use this workbook

1. Complete as many entries as possible for each chapter.

2. Not all spaces need to be filled, move on when you have exhausted the information for the chapter.

3. Complete the Review page at the end to bring the information together.

4. Notes Pages and optional activities are located after the Chapter Pages. Use them to record any information not covered in the Chapter Pages.

5. Notes on the author can be kept on pages 4 and 5.

Need a Teachers Guide created?

Upgrade to the Lessons on Demand line of books!

Send requests and questions to Johndavidpennington@yahoo.com

Author Notes

* Place any information about the author here.

Before Reading Questions

What is the reason for reading this book?

What do you already know about this book?

What, based on the cover, do you think this book is about?

Before Reading Questions

Have you read any other books by this author?

Is this book part of a series? If so what are the other books?

What are you looking forward to when reading this book?

* After Reading questions can be found in the back.

NAME:

TEACHER:

Date:

Chapters/Pages

Events
1.
2.
3.
4.
5.

*_Not all number lines will have answers._

Characters
1.
2.
3.
4.
5.
6.

Possible Future Events
1.
2.

Locations
1.
2.

Key Terms / Vocabulary
1.
2.
3.
4.

Conflicts / Problems
1.
2.
3.
4.

Main Idea

NAME:

TEACHER:

Date:

Chapters/Pages

* <u>Not all number lines will have answers.</u>

Characters

1.

2.

3.

4.

5.

6.

Locations

1.

2.

Conflicts / Problems

1.

2.

3.

4.

Events

1.

2.

3.

4.

5.

Possible Future Events

1.

2.

Key Terms / Vocabulary

1.

2.

3.

4.

Main Idea

NAME:

TEACHER:

Date:

Precognition Sheet (guess)

Who ?

What's going to happen?

What will be the result?

Who ?

What's going to happen?

What will be the result?

Who ?

What's going to happen?

What will be the result?

Who ?

What's going to happen?

What will be the result?

How many did you get correct?

NAME:

TEACHER:

Date:

Chapters/Pages

* <u>Not all number lines will have answers.</u>

Characters

1.

2.

3.

4.

5.

6.

Locations

1.

2.

Conflicts / Problems

1.

2.

3.

4.

Events

1.

2.

3.

4.

5.

Possible Future Events

1.

2.

Key Terms / Vocabulary

1.

2.

3.

4.

Main Idea

NAME:

TEACHER:

Date:

Chapters/Pages

Events

1.

2.

3.

4.

5.

* <u>Not all number lines will have answers.</u>

Characters

1.

2.

3.

4.

5.

6.

Possible Future Events

1.

2.

Key Terms / Vocabulary

1.

2.

3.

4.

Locations

1.

2.

Conflicts / Problems

1.

2.

3.

4.

Main Idea

NAME:

TEACHER:

Date:

Chapters/Pages

Events

1.

2.

3.

4.

5.

* <u>Not all number lines will have answers.</u>

Characters

1.

2.

3.

4.

5.

6.

Possible Future Events

1.

2.

Key Terms / Vocabulary

1.

2.

3.

4.

Locations

1.

2.

Conflicts / Problems

1.

2.

3.

4.

Main Idea

NAME:

TEACHER:

Date:

Chapters/Pages

* Not all number lines will have answers.

Characters

1.
2.
3.
4.
5.
6.

Locations

1.
2.

Conflicts / Problems

1.
2.
3.
4.

Events

1.
2.
3.
4.
5.

Possible Future Events

1.
2.

Key Terms / Vocabulary

1.
2.
3.
4.

Main Idea

NAME:

TEACHER:

Date:

Chapters/Pages

* <u>Not all number lines will have answers.</u>

Characters

1.

2.

3.

4.

5.

6.

Locations

1.

2.

Conflicts / Problems

1.

2.

3.

4.

Events

1.

2.

3.

4.

5.

Possible Future Events

1.

2.

Key Terms / Vocabulary

1.

2.

3.

4.

Main Idea

NAME:

TEACHER:

Date:

Chapters/Pages

Events
1.
2.
3.
4.
5.

* Not all number lines will have answers.

Characters
1.
2.
3.
4.
5.
6.

Possible Future Events
1.
2.

Locations
1.
2.

Key Terms / Vocabulary
1.
2.
3.
4.

Conflicts / Problems
1.
2.
3.
4.

Main Idea

NAME:

TEACHER:

Date:

Chapters/Pages

* <u>Not all number lines will have answers.</u>

Characters

1.

2.

3.

4.

5.

6.

Locations

1.

2.

Conflicts / Problems

1.

2.

3.

4.

Events

1.

2.

3.

4.

5.

Possible Future Events

1.

2.

Key Terms / Vocabulary

1.

2.

3.

4.

Main Idea

NAME:

TEACHER:

Date:

Chapters/Pages

Events

1.

2.

3.

4.

5.

* <u>Not all number lines will have answers.</u>

Characters

1.

2.

3.

4.

5.

6.

Possible Future Events

1.

2.

Key Terms / Vocabulary

1.

2.

3.

4.

Locations

1.

2.

Conflicts / Problems

1.

2.

3.

4.

Main Idea

NAME:

TEACHER:

Date:

Chapters/Pages

* <u>Not all number lines will have answers.</u>

Characters

1.
2.
3.
4.
5.
6.

Locations

1.
2.

Conflicts / Problems

1.
2.
3.
4.

Events

1.
2.
3.
4.
5.

Possible Future Events

1.
2.

Key Terms / Vocabulary

1.
2.
3.
4.

Main Idea

What parts of the book were the most enjoyable?

Which characters were your favorite and why?

Write a summary of the book.

What are the 5 most important events?

Write a review of the book.

What is likely to be a plot to the next book?

Draw an advertisement for the book

Character Sketch

Name

Draw a picture

Personality/ Distinguishing marks

Connections to other characters

Important Actions

Character Sketch

Name

Personality/ Distinguishing marks

Draw a picture

Connections to other characters

Important Actions

Character Sketch

Name

Personality/ Distinguishing marks

Draw a picture

Connections to other characters

Important Actions

Character Sketch

Name

Personality/ Distinguishing marks

Draw a picture

Connections to other characters

Important Actions

Character Sketch

Name

Personality/ Distinguishing marks

Draw a picture

Connections to other characters

Important Actions

Character Sketch

Name

Personality/ Distinguishing marks

Draw a picture

Connections to other characters

Important Actions

Character Sketch

Name

Draw a picture

Personality/ Distinguishing marks

Connections to other characters

Important Actions

Character Sketch

Name

Personality/ Distinguishing marks

Draw a picture

Connections to other characters

Important Actions

Character Sketch

Name

Personality/ Distinguishing marks

Draw a picture

Connections to other characters

Important Actions

Character Sketch

Name

Personality/ Distinguishing marks

Draw a picture

Connections to other characters

Important Actions

Character Sketch

Name

Draw a picture

Personality/ Distinguishing marks

Connections to other characters

Important Actions

Character Sketch

Name

Personality/ Distinguishing marks

Draw a picture

Connections to other characters

Important Actions

Character Sketch

Name

Personality/ Distinguishing marks

Draw a picture

Connections to other characters

Important Actions

Character Sketch

Name

Personality/ Distinguishing marks

Draw a picture

Connections to other characters

Important Actions

Character Sketch

Name

Draw a picture

Personality/ Distinguishing marks

Connections to other characters

Important Actions

Compare and Contrast

Venn Diagram

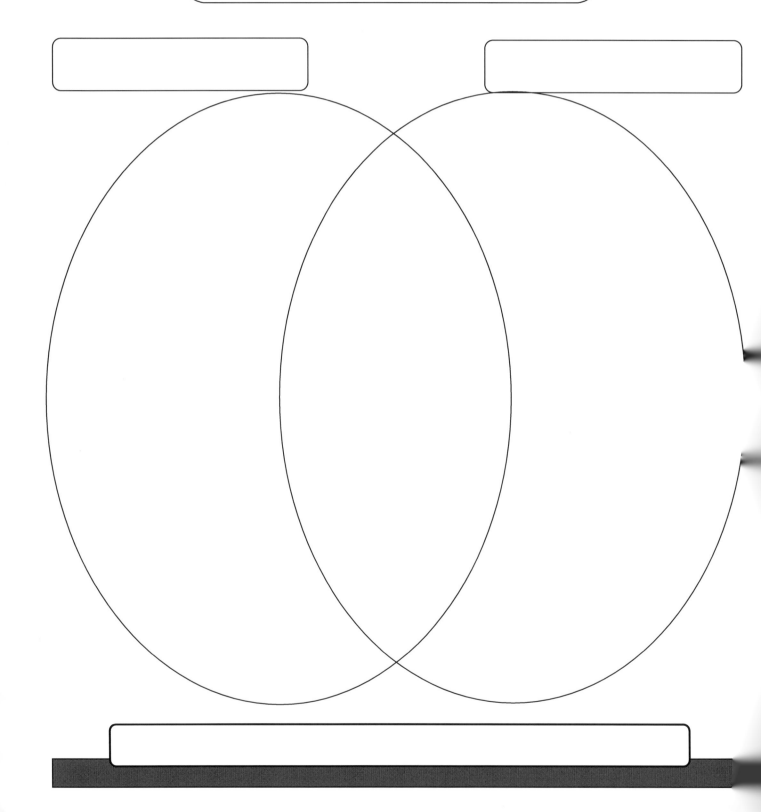

Notes

NAME:

TEACHER:

Date:

Character Sketch

Name

Draw a picture

Personality/ Distinguishing marks

Connections to other characters

Important Actions

NAME:

TEACHER:

Date:

Comic Strip

NAME:

TEACHER:

Date:

Draw the Scene: What five things have you included in the scene?

1   2   3

4   5

NAME:

TEACHER:

Date:

Interview: Who _____

Question:

Answer:

Question:

Answer:

Question:

Answer:

Question:

Answer:

NAME:

TEACHER:

Date:

Lost Scene: Write a scene that takes place between _____ and
_____

Making Connections

What is the connection?

NAME:

TEACHER:

Date:

Research connections

Source (URL, Book, Magazine, Interview)

What am I researching?

Facts I found that could be useful or notes

1.

2.

3.

4.

5.

6.

NAME:

TEACHER:

Date:

Sequencing or timeline

1.

2.

3.

4.

5.

NAME:

TEACHER:

Date:

Support This!

Supporting text

What page?

Supporting text

What page?

Central idea or statement

Supporting text

What page?

Supporting text

What page?

NAME:

TEACHER:

Date:

Travel Brochure

Why should you visit?

What are you going to see?

Map

Special Events

Notes

NAME:

TEACHER:

Date:

* <u>Not all number lines will have answers.</u>

Main Characters

1.
2.
3.
4.
5.
6.
7.
8.
9.
10.
11.
12.
13.
14.
15.
16.
17.
18.

Important Locations

1.
2.
3.
4.
5.

Resolved Conflicts / Problems

1.
2.
3.
4.
5.
6.
7.
8.
9.
10.
11.
12.

Most Important Events

1.
2.
3.
4.
5.
6.
7.
8.
9.
10.

Main Idea of the Novel

Unresolved Conflicts / Problems

1.
2.
3.
4.
5.
6.
7.
8.
9.
10.
11.
12.

Possible Future Events

1.
2.
3.
4.
5.
6.

Manufactured by Amazon.ca
Bolton, ON